Free Verse Editions

Edited by Jon Thompson

WONDER ROOMS

ALLISON FUNK

*For Anna —
who, like me,
is drawn to wonders
found in rooms
and beyond —
with thanks for
your poems and
friendship,*
Allison
Feb. 2018

Parlor Press
Anderson, South Carolina
www.parlorpress.com

Parlor Press LLC, Anderson, South Carolina, 29621

Printed in the United States of America
S A N: 2 5 4 - 8 8 7 9

Library of Congress Cataloging-in-Publication Data

Funk, Allison.
   [Poems. Selections]
   Wonder rooms / Allison Funk.
      pages ; cm. -- (Free verse editions)
   ISBN 978-1-60235-618-4 (softcover : acid-free paper)
   I. Title.
   PS3556.U62A6 2015
   811'.54--dc23
                              2015002990
Cover design by Josh Reingold
Cover art by Sheldon Helfman. Used by permission.

Printed on acid-free paper.

1 2 3 4 5

Parlor Press, LLC is an independent publisher of scholarly and
trade titles in print and multimedia formats. This book is available
in paperback and ebook formats from Parlor Press on the World
Wide Web at http://www.parlorpress.com or through online and
brick-and-mortar bookstores. For submission information or to
find out about Parlor Press publications, write to Parlor Press, 3015
Brackenberry Drive, Anderson, South Carolina, 29621, or email
editor@parlorpress.com.

Contents

The Anteroom   5
Wonder Rooms   6
Inside Imperato's *Camera delle Meraviglie*   7
Leviathan   8
The Fallout Shelter   9
In The Enlightenment Room at the British Museum   10
When My Son Jumped Into the East River to Save New York
    from a Bomb   11
Nautilus pompilius   12
When I 302'd Him in Pennsylvania   13
In which rooms do we put what we can't stand to remember?   14
Ménerbes   15
This Dark   19
In the Pentlands   20
The Seven Chambers of Teresa of Avila's *Interior Castle*   21
Fontaine-de-Vaucluse   28
Snorkeling   30
Asp   32
Into the *Chambres* of Dora Maar   33
North Bridge   40
Tempo   41
ICU   43
Maria Sibylla Merian's Metamorphoses   44
6 rue de Savoie, Paris   52
Basilisk   53
On a Few Lines by Rilke   54
Loci   55
A Flight of Stairs   57

Notes   59
Acknowledgments   61
About the Author   63
Free Verse Editions   65

WONDER ROOMS

If at times, through the long night, I trouble you
with my urgent knocking—
this is why: I hear you breathe so seldom.
I know you're all alone in that room.

—Rainer Maria Rilke

The Anteroom

It's murky inside.

Dim as an old painting
half-hidden under dust and darkened varnish.

Still, I recognize her in the gloom.

Daughter, I want to say,

for her silence is so familiar I'm in the cellar
of her chest. Lodged in her throat.
What can't be swallowed

or escaped.
I know it as she does, weight

and counterweight. Every syllable
a heavy step laboring
up a narrow, twisting stair.
At the top: a locked door.

With a cinder alive on my tongue,
I tell her I will listen.

I'll copy her fragments down.

Wonder Rooms

Though ordinary in their own habitats, introduced to one another,
    Alligator to polar bear,

Ostrich and starfish, they became a bestiary like none other on earth.
    A country found nowhere

On maps. The tusk of a narwhal, a dodo bird, mermaid's hand.
    In a wonder room,

More dream than museum, collectors could travel
    To their own Interior.

Room within rooms, within. Kingdom, Phylum, Class, Family,
    Genus, Species.

And so I gathered them along a roadway in France. *Cernuella, Virgata*
    Clinging to a blade of grass

Or in clusters sometimes, small versions of the grapes ready for picking,
    Though not the Syrah's blue-rouge.

Pearly grey instead, these slightly flattened globes. Their orbits
    Inscribed upon them.

So what if they're only *limaçons?* Common vineyard snails.
    My room

Is becoming the field they came from: a Milky Way
    Studded with them.

Inside Imperato's *Camera delle Meraviglie*

Naples, 1599

Ferrante Imperato directs us to look up
as if to the constellations,
though crustaceans swim above us instead.
Starfish and moon snails.
When we ask, he identifies cockles and conch
among the flying fish—
fans, he says, of water and air.
Meanwhile his son, Francesco,
with a pointer the length of his arm,
aims at a crocodile where a chandelier
should hang. Chameleon and flamingo,
sea urchin and seal, uncanny the face
of what's that creature looking down at us?
Have we lost our compass?
On what axis are we spinning
in this eely otherworld—
not knowing, all of a sudden, what writhes
or flies. What's here. Far?
Silent now, our guide
leans against a window's diamond pane
in the ebbing light of his wonder room
as if to say how thin it is between.

Leviathan

from the Myrrour of the Worlde *by William Caxton, 1481*

After my son pummeled the back door,
fisted a knife into the lock,

spat and stabbed at the glass between us,
after the police came, cuffed him,

and left, I tried, still trembling, to remember
how even the children of gods misbehaved.

In all the creation tales I've known,
floods are raised out of the fantasy

parents have of starting over,
their vision of a beach swept clean

of mussels and whelks,
even the little webbed prints

gulls and terns leave in their wakes.
It's tempting to pretend,

lured by story or song,
but easier to believe in the leviathan,

that staple of medieval bestiaries
sailors mistook for an island.

Who can blame them for their delusions?
No wonder, exhausted by storms,

they might see an enormous floating back
and confuse it for land. At sea so long, *No end,*

no end, they might even have been relieved
when the whale dove, taking them down.

The Fallout Shelter

You go back sometimes
to when you thought you could survive
in a cinderblock room. Or chose to believe
your father who built it. Your mother
who stocked the makeshift shelves
with canned goods, matches and blankets.
Brothers who chose games
to play until you heard the all-clear.

Allee, allee all in free.

Come out from where you've been hiding.

In The Enlightenment Room
at the British Museum

nothing's alive
      except those of us drawn to what's kept
    in cabinets, the fading, threadbare,
severed or stuffed—

the Superb, for example, or Magnificent
      feathered blue and snow, the fickle golds
    of sunset, dawn's pastels, *of* this world,
but not,

reasoned Europeans far from New Guinea
      where (how could they know?)
    traders removed the birds' feet.
Think

if we never touched down, lived like a cloud
      in between. *Paradise,*
    someone sighed, weary of his own to-and-fros,
his on and on

over cobble and acre.
      And so he christened the Lesser and Greater
    for the first realm he felt exiled from—
a sanctuary

not altogether unlike this,
      where beasts (unburdened by breath)
    and (downed) fowl coexist
and are named.

When My Son Jumped Into the East River to Save New York from a Bomb

I tried to remember how he'd learned to swim—
    I must have taught him—
but trying to remember reminded me of squinting
    at a line of optometrist's letters,
that fuzz of recognition that clears or disappears
    blink by blink.
What I did remember was how at seven or eight
    he loved diving from the high board,
how I never took my eyes off the spot
    where he'd gone in
before he surfaced, seal-slick, hunting praise.
    And as one memory bears another
I'm back at the ocean the day
    lifeguards waved everyone out—
hurricane warnings—
    breakers swelling, clouds wheeling
like murmurations of starlings
    as my son waded farther away from shore,
ignoring my cries until in the slantwise rain,
    when he could barely stand,
he turned around.
    In between so much is curtained.
Even when the letters come into focus,
    sharp as any lens can render,
they spell nothing that makes sense.

Nautilus pompilius

When I think of it descending
   along cliffs of coral,
      I sink, subtracting years
the nautilus, unlike us,
   would have put behind,
      sealing each chamber up
when outgrown
   to create another
      more spacious one,
an opalescence of fractals
   mysterious to me as the Golden Mean
      or Sacred Geometry,
this cephalopod (feet where it's headed,
   pinholes for eyes)
      that won't go looking
for trouble and knows enough
   when it's there
      to shut the door.

When I 302'd Him in Pennsylvania

It came to mind that 302 was my area code
    when I was a child,
        and the numbers began to blur. Which

had I called to reach the crisis center?
    Had he shown he was unable to care
        for himself for 30 days? 30 years, yes,

I'd answered, misunderstanding.
    How many minutes had it taken
        from the time of my call

for police officers to arrive and cuff my son?
    And, once admitted, how long
        could the hospital keep him?

Was it 120 hours unless a judge approved
    a 303 extending commitment for a period
        not to exceed how many days?

Would a 304b allow further treatment?
    A 305 obtain another 180 days? Even then,
        Act 77 of 1975—or was it '76—

might let him appeal for the right
    to possess a gun.
        I didn't know

after I'd read the petition
    in a thunderstorm, signed,
        then hidden in my car

as he was taken away,
    I didn't know how soon
        they'd let him go.

In which rooms do we put what we can't stand to remember?

In his memory palace, Matteo Ricci
     kept his rooms spacious and clean
          so he could locate what they held
easily in his mind.

To forget, you crowd yours instead,

     mound what you want gone
          like the dead heaped one on top of another,
none of them marked by a stone.

No signposts like Ricci's
     two warriors locked in combat
          or the women he stationed in corners— northeast,
southwest.

Create a blueprint, he taught, so you never get lost
     in your thoughts.

     But when you feel you might lose your mind
by retracing your steps—

what came first, what happened next,
     the worst—
          you open your rooms to rain
and the blinding sun,

bid grief goodbye,
     chaff for a breeze.

     Bring it on, even a twister, you cry,
to be free of what is inside.

Ménerbes

How to speak freedom, my surprise, at the end of a thousand detours:
there is no bottom, there is no ceiling.

—René Char

I.

The moon is about to rise through a parasol pine.
　　Soon the perched villages will constellate the ridges
　　　　like votives in the darkening abbey of Sénanque

where the monks sing vespers:
　　Bienheureux ceux qui pleurent,
　　　　Car ils seront consolés.

　　　　It could be the twelfth century.

Blessed are those who mourn:
　　the robed who tend their lavender acres,
　　　　women kneeling in prayer,

　　　　　even the likes of me

tracing the marks of masons in medieval stone,
　　A and *J* and *M* and * and +
　　　　as if I could find my name.

II.

Here, *here* is the door.
  And just inside, honeyed by southern light,
    the room that's mine for a month.

I call it, after René Char,
  "la chambre dans l'espace"
    it seems so spacious

with its oversized mirror doubling
  an arm chair upholstered in white linen,
    a divan large enough for lovemaking,

and the fireplace *en face.*
  May the mirror multiply
    what I bring to this room as well, I wish,

moving to a window that looks out
  at the Luberon range and, between,
    a valley of vineyards, orchards

and groves of *oliviers* with their fruit still green—
  the olives that, come December, will ripen
    into what the Romans called black pearls.

III.

Once, when I was a girl, I wrote my name over and over,
    each Allison lined up under another
        until I didn't know who I was.

Here, to fix images in my mind more surely
    than words on the page,
        I take the path I have for weeks—

past the chapel of Notre Dame des Grâces
    and down the slope to the vineyards
        where workers under umbrellas

pick row upon row of grapes.
    Behind me now: the village
        lodged in a cliff, medieval, still,

still there even as Mont Ventoux disappears
    in a noon's haze, that chalky light
        distinct from dawn's silvering mist.

Nothing is wider than this.

IV.

One night, fists against my shutters,
    it knocked and knocked.
        Sacré mistral!

I answered the damned wind
    as if it were my familiar,
        a family member, god forbid.

If I could build my house
    I'd choose one like those in Provence
        that face south,

away from the blast
    that crosses the Rhône
        and topples grown women

before clearing the sky
    and cooling the vines.
        Bow down, the cypress gestured.

Stand guard, the plane trees mimed in rows.
    And wrought
        to let the mistral pass right through,

the open belfry towered
    without ceiling or walls.
        All night while I kept vigil

I heard the hours ring.

This Dark

It seemed that out of battle I escaped
Down some profound dull tunnel . . . .

        —Wilfred Owen, "Strange Meeting"

In the time they had
   between walls lit by guttering candles
and the glint of pickaxes tap-tapping at grit,

   the Germans and British tunneled
below the craters of No Man's Land
   carrying fuses and bombs.

Afraid of meeting his enemy under ground
   a Brit would drive a stick
into dirt, bite the end, and listen

   with his tongue for vibrations.
Even then, he could meet a German
   tunneling toward him. Clay-stained

features bleared, the same fatigue—
   except for their uniforms,
who could tell the men apart?

   In his mind's bleak pathways,
my son, who has never been a soldier,
   fears the enemy he does not recognize

as himself. Wars begin
   within such tunnels.
And in their winding ends

   I can hardly bear to find the umbilical,
but there it is: a dark hall connecting us
   all. The blood. The waste.

In the Pentlands

outside Edinburgh

Here, where I am buffeted,
    barely able to stand,
a kestrel hangs
    impossibly still in the wind.
I envy its otherness,
    its look of being somewhere else—

far from where I've scrabbled
    up the slope, unloosening scree
as I climbed, lacking altogether
    the grace of this hawk
becalmed in mid air. *Becalmed*
    despite gusts strong enough
to rend a sail in the firth,
    that blue hem
at the end of these hills.

    I want down
without tripping over moles
    tunneling their runways
under my feet. Sheep, stones, shrew
    half-hidden in the upland grasses—
everyone tilting toward sea level,
    exposed as the skylark
and golden plover that veer
    in the airspace between Scald Law
and the kestrel's barely quivering wings.

    It's a recurring dream
I have of hovering, the calm
    I call kestrel in this storm.
Waking, I know even the bird's lift
    is short-lived. The hair's-breadth
between heather and heath,
    those seconds before it plunges
headlong into a vole.

The Seven Chambers of Teresa of Avila's *Interior Castle*

The First

In a room flooded
with sunlight, I cannot see
through the earth in my eyes:

    dirt, grit, dust—

how it stains, sullies—the shame
of it—soil, loam, soot, muck.

    : :

Second

When I heard nothing, it was no trial
to remain silent.

Selfsame.
                    Here

though it's no louder
than scurries of mice,

cough, sigh, caught
breath, step,

restless fingers smoothing wool,

                    though the call
is piecemeal

(stray words, pollen on the wind)

            my ear is a vestibule.

        : :

Third

What am I waiting for?

With the wind and snow and bad roads,
it can only get worse.
And yet I inch.
Unspool my thread.

       A fearful, foolhardy stumbler

until I remember
the globe of my soul
dizzy in its orbit

may spin free
the longer I stand
on my knees.

    : :

Fourth

Out of what's parched:

                      a girl—

                            in petticoats.

           And over them

velvet
silk

           water-becoming
ribbons

               fold upon fold

                     gathering sheen.

Holy Holy

           the headlong plunge

to where it sweetly
pools.

      : :

The Fifth

An iota.

At rest.

: :

Sixth

If, in this crevice,
the sleep of the unborn could last

                          but
          what's that pulse?

A wick is lit,

and in its spill

a cubbyhole, cupboard, closet open,

but dead-end.

          Fire, Nectar,

bless me with the spaciousness of a dome

or a cell of honeycomb.

The longed-for door.

    : :

At Last

And. And.

And. So much

when it rains
                        who can tell the river

from the downpour?

Fontaine-de-Vaucluse

Where does it end? she asks
before she's lured below the surface
of what's welling up inside her

by the river where Cousteau,
diving ten, twenty, nearly fifty meters
down, explored room after room of a spring
so labyrinthine no one has found its source.

Like opening a door
that yields to another, the next,
she thinks,

then, far from home,
finds one ajar
she thought she'd forgotten.

Going inside,
she returns to a single hour
in the cavernous space of Grand Central

where a clock's four faces seemed to power
people between destinations,
as though there wasn't time for indecision
or a change in direction.

Had she looked up and seen
the zodiac glowing overhead
before descending the terminal's stairs,
would she have found bodies to navigate by?

No, no,
the galaxy in gold leaf
wasn't revealed until later.
Then it was only a ceiling covered with soot.
An overcast night.

Still, shouldn't she have known
when he turned to her in the Whispering Gallery?

If not there, then in their slow
kiss before she boarded the Silver Meteor?

Yes,
it should have been clear (even though
they were young and he was her first lover).

She would make the mistake on her own.
She would come to regret it later.

Snorkeling

What if, late in my life,
    an old love returned?
        I might get carried away

as I did my first time in that otherworld
    ablaze with coney
        and neon blue tang,

soundless except for the resonance
    of my breath, a hypnotic
        one-two, now/then, why not

love me. I must have seen
    the stoplight parrotfish
        beam red from a grotto,

but, heedless, sped up,
    flippers propelling me over coral
        resembling Gaudí's Sagrada Família

still unfinished after a hundred years.
    Remembering,
        I circled the remains

of countless marine animals.
    Fragile memorials, yes,
        but not harmless I'd learn:

the thousand mouths of the reef
    that open out of hunger,
        alive to the careless swimmer

who comes too close.
    One who, succumbing to the pull
        of the beautiful, swims out

so far she finds herself at the mercy
   of surf that flings her
      against the stinging ridge.

Cells meeting cells, tentacles, flesh,
   she's left with the mark
      of a fiery ring that burns longer

than a slap. Weeks. Months.
   A tattoo that may never fade
      from the soft underside of her arm.

Asp

from an illustration in The Aberdeen Bestiary, *12th century*

In the King James Version
the asp, who is a she, will not hearken
to the voice of charmers and so *stops her ear.*

Drawn, she seems to press one
against the ground while plugging
the other ear with her tail

to avoid the enchantments of the human
armed with a stick and a shield
in the illuminated manuscript
of Aberdeen's bestiary.

How else is a girl to survive
if she doesn't know the gift
of her poison?

Listen, she's always told,

she who will share her Kingdom
(after Linnaeus) with *Vipera,*
a creature, it turns out,

that has no ears you can see.
They're interior, though,
akin to what, in women,
we call intuition.

Use your own
and you may understand
the plum-colored asp

has spun herself into a wheel
ready to roll away.

Into the *Chambres* of Dora Maar

His voice nearly gone
                    (add enough water and pigment thins)

she's listening to the plainsong
of doves in the garden,

                    their *you   you   you*

calling her slowly back to herself
until she's jarred by laughter coming from

                              who is it

below her window facing the Avenue du Général Baron Robert?

Footsteps. Three knocks at the heavy front door—

                                        where
is the quiet she's come to Provence for?

        : :

Nighttime

the village belfry wakes her,

                    bell that rings the hour
twice, so it's 12 a.m.

            12 a.m. again.

When finally she falls back to sleep she's young —
the beauty she was in the Thirties.

So how can she be in Ménerbes rifling through her closet?
These—how can they be her clothes?

This wardrobe of an old woman
who'd cover her white with a wig.

And now, aware she's wearing nothing,
she frantically parts one dress from the next

until, suddenly, they open onto a scene, a play going on.
Someone shouts at her from the wings to

                    Get off the stage

and she's in a madhouse fleeing hands
nearly upon her.

Her pearls, where has she left them?

And the phone won't it stop ringing?

     : :

Dawn,

and for moments,
                 motionless,

she's just a figure in Picasso's paintings.

             How can a woman keep from disappearing?

In her apartment in Paris at 6 rue de Savoie
she placed mirrors in every room,
on walls, mantelpiece, inside walk-in closets,

seeking herself in each—

especially the convex looking glass
where her face loomed,
filling the frame.

     : :

29 rue d'Astorg.

Her first studio.

       Also a photograph by Dora Maar, *surréaliste.*

What she'd been
before Picasso convinced her to give up
her camera for a brush.

In the center, an *objet trouvé*

               found trashed, a doll
neither child nor woman quite.

Under a loose-fitting dress,
the beginning of a breast.

Elsewhere, vestiges of baby fat: round knees, chubby hands.

Odd enough, but what would she have if she broke the head off?

      Not *Dora,*

famous for her face, darling of the Surrealists,
Man Ray, Paul Éluard, Breton,

             this grotesque

whose neck is a chicken bone
gnawed clean.

She gives the headless one
a single eye and, for a mouth, a blunt line
that resembles a beak where the neck ends.

Then pulling a sleeve down on one side
to expose a shoulder,

she poses the creature before an image of Versailles' orangery,
so its long hall comes to resemble a birth canal.

Oh, what she's mothered!

She who will never have a child of her own.

: :

And the route she took
to *l'Hôpital Sainte-Anne?*

Quickly before the past is erased!

Before doctors attach electrodes to her temples.
Before she convulses, loses consciousness—

record all the sun-filled streets and darkrooms
where she learned the photographer's art,

the Seine at dusk, lovers

before Picasso, rations, curfews, occupation,
the lance of his affection for Marie-Thérèse, Françoise

and *la femme qui pleure,*
that woman he took her for—
not *Dora,*

though how could she be sure
now that everything had the blank look

of starched linen? And in her head, she kept repeating
the final steps in printing—
stop, fix—
as if she were praying.

Turn to God,

her doctor advised—for you it's that
or the straitjacket.

: :

Sur le tard.

But not too late.

What she's waited for.

Not the end of day or gloaming.
More like the cooling hours of afternoon.

All those hair-raising, harebrained, hairpin turns
she takes alone on her motorbike in the mountains,

strands of gray loosened by the dry
Provençal wind escaping her scarf.

Faster, faster—olive grove, orchard, vineyard,
the black cicada that brings luck in the summer—

everything's ripening
for her watercolors.

: :

Meditation, she came to believe,

was like a shutter (camera, window)
opened and left open

until, with her eyes closed,
she could see Mont Ventoux.

Sky and Mountain. Landscape and Sky. Large White Sky.

She'd name her paintings of what she saw,

though like the monks at vespers
singing of *les cieux et les cieux des cieux*

she'd learned language was important only in so far
as it became transparent—
a lens to see through.

     : :

It was said she became more and more reclusive
because she was no longer beautiful.
That she was afraid to show her ruined face.

But she didn't live in that face anymore—

Picasso's bird-woman, Sphinx,
harpy to his minotaur.

How far away the dramas of other people
seemed as she looked out from her ridge
to the valley below,
                         vineyard and orchard blurring,

the steep path she'd taken down to the chapel of Notre Dame des Grâces
obscured by a morning's mist.

It wasn't madness, fear, or sadness that confined her.

Inside, tubes of pigment covered her studio tables:
Numbers 46, 74, 16, 13.

The *jaune soufre, vert Romain clair,*
rouge de Chine, and *bleu outremer*

others would find when they turned a key in her lock
and, in the light invading Dora Maar's rooms,

discovered canvases strung from the walls,
a cross made of wooden stretchers, photos she'd returned to,

and a notebook of poems.

What no one would find, she'd written,
was *pale yellow*—

the tint for her of what was interior.

North Bridge

A woman beyond middle age
waits on a bridge for a bus,
at peace in a solitude
that polishes every surface:

the steel girders that span
Old Town and New,
the railing she leans against,
headlights in the distance.

She's in Edinburgh,
but could be anywhere,
for isn't it in the nature
of the miraculous to be released?

She'll try to remember this night
wherever she is afterwards
with the moon full above her
like a glassmaker's bubble

or a silver-white pod of lunaria.
Even when someone calls it
a common moonwort,
and transcendence

comes to resemble a note
that lasts only as long
as a breath,
she'll tell herself to take another.

Tempo

My brother is driving me to the airport
    when I ask him to do his cricket imitations.
        Close your eyes, he says,

but I still can't tell second violins from first.
    Think of each as a soloist,
        wings like a bow and strings,

he insists. Maybe
    it will help to pretend
        he's guiding me through stands

of cattails along the Chesapeake,
    whispering *tinnulenta,*
        tinnula,

tinnulacita,
    his names for the slow, faster,
        and fastest new species he's found,

or, gaining speed on the interstate,
    to remember him as a boy
        listening for crickets

from inside his room,
    lights out, windows open
        on sticky summer nights.

Now he's saying it's natural
    to lose some high notes
        with aging—

soon, he worries,
    he'll have trouble himself
        telling the crickets apart.

For the time being, though,
  my brother is trilling beside me,
   the wind's blowing in

as it does across Still Pond Creek
  where his crickets thrive,
   and on a warm day in autumn

I want to slow it down, way down,
  this, our time
   between arrival and farewell.

ICU

I can't sleep in this room

with the ventilator honking,
feeding tube dripping.
Alarms triggered by the rising and falling
cadence of a heart.

But he can. My son found three stories down.

No one is able to wake him.

Don't think of Icarus, there wasn't a moment
of joy in this.

More like the story of the labyrinth.
A minotaur in the middle of his head.

When they asked who was the next of kin,
I could have said it is his inheritance,

the nightmare of not speaking,
of words fleeing into parts unknown,
him chasing after through thicket, woods, windbreak—

even his mother unable to catch him.

Maria Sibylla Merian's Metamorphoses

1647

Not from dew. Not from cheese or wool.
Not from rain, hair or horse dung.

Not from cabbage. Cobwebs. Sweet basil.
Vapor. Oxen or mules.

Not spontaneous generation.
But metamorphosis? In insects?

Nature's lowliest. Unseemly.
Even unholy. Not unlike Satan

twisting into a woman,
witches multiplying like maggots.

1664

With a mortar and pestle
she ground, she mixed pigments.

    Not from dew. Not from cheese or wool.
    Not from rain, hair or horse dung.

Green from the buckthorn's sap,
gold scraped from mouths of volcanoes.

    Not from cabbage. Cobwebs. Sweet basil.
    Vapor. Oxen or mules.

On lilies and hyacinth,
she'd find larvae to raise.

    Not *spontaneous generation.*
    But metamorphosis? In insects?

Some with blue arrows down their backs,
others dusted yellow and snow.

    Nature's lowliest. Unseemly.
    Even unholy. Not unlike Satan.

What's more amazing
than a pupa swaddled like a child?

    Twisting into a woman,
    witches multiplying like maggots?

46

1670

Female painters?
Guilds bolted Germany's doors.

*With a mortar and pestle
she ground, she mixed pigments.*

She studied the pupa that frees
itself from its case,

*green from the buckthorn's sap,
gold scraped from mouths of volcanoes.*

Were the household chores never finished,
the spinning of wool into yarn?

*On lilies and hyacinth
she'd find larvae to raise.*

Along muddy banks, alone in her garden,
she followed the insects' fruity scent,

*some with blue arrows down their backs,
others dusted yellow and snow.*

With the care she'd take with her daughters,
she tended each chrysalis.

*What's more amazing
than a pupa swaddled like a child?*

1680

The larva, a spirit; the pupa,
a girl; imago, full grown and ready to fly.

> *Female painters?*
> *Guilds bolted Germany's doors.*

Reliquaries—the *Wunderkammern*
housing insects fuzzed with dust.

> *She studied the pupa that frees*
> *itself from its case.*

She fed them sugared water, the newborn
Garden Tiger, Hawk moth, and Emperor.

> *Were the household chores never finished,*
> *the spinning of wool into yarn?*

With brushes tipped with marten or sable
she painted molt after molt.

> *Along muddy banks, alone in her garden,*
> *she followed the insects' fruity scent*

beyond the camphor of wonder rooms
and their musty habitats.

> *With the care she'd take with her daughters,*
> *she tended each chrysalis.*

1692

What if she found species
no European had seen?

 The larva, a spirit; the pupa,
 a girl; imago, full grown and ready to fly.

Not divided in boxes, moths from cocoons.
The White Witch drying its wings.

 Reliquaries—the Wunderkammern
 housing insects fuzzed with dust.

From which plants did they lift,
which return to, to feed?

 She fed them sugared water, the newborn
 Garden Tiger, Hawk moth, and Emperor

she'd record in *The Caterpillar's*
Wondrous Metamorphosis.

 With brushes tipped with marten or sable
 she painted molt after molt.

Frankfurt, Nuremberg, Amsterdam.
In the New World, what might she become

 beyond the camphor of wonder rooms
 and their musty habitats?

1699

Far from what she'd known.
Surinam. Unmapped. Interior.

> *What if she found species*
> *no European had seen?*

Caterpillars turning crimson
and cream in the guava's leaves,

> *not divided in boxes, moths from cocoons.*
> *The White Witch drying its wings*

glimpsed through a blur
of heat or rain.

> *From which plants did they lift,*
> *which return to, to feed?*

A tarantula. Leaf-cutter ants,
larvae with venomous spines

> *she'd record in* The Metamorphosis
> of the Insects of Surinam.

Uncased, wings stretched
wide as a woman's hand.

> *Frankfurt, Nuremberg, Amsterdam.*
> *In the New World, what might she become?*

1700

Spider-like: the strangler vines,
webbed trees, the tail ends of monkeys

> *far from what she'd known.*
> *Surinam. Unmapped. Interior.*

Species teeming
from canopy to floor,

> *caterpillars turning crimson*
> *and cream in the guava's leaves.*

Seen through a fever,
a flash of azure

> *glimpsed through a blur*
> *of heat or rain,*

glints of carmine, indigo,
ochre and ultramarine.

> *A tarantula. Leaf-cutter ants,*
> *larvae with venomous spines,*

a Blue Morpho,
Sphinx moth, Ghost

> *uncased. Wings stretched*
> *wide as a woman's hand.*

1717

Spider-like: the strangler vines,
webbed trees, the tail ends of monkeys,

species teeming
from canopy to floor.

Seen through a fever,
a flash of azure,

glints of carmine, indigo,
ochre and ultramarine:

her Blue Morpho,
Sphinx moth. Ghost.

6 rue de Savoie, Paris

Dora Maar, 1907-1997

Come in

(though she's gone, and would not have asked me if she were here).

Yes, I've invited myself, and, inside, see me mirrored everywhere: on the walls, above the mantelpiece, in closets, storage rooms, in the eye of her Rolleiflex, the silver plated frame into which she looked to photograph herself lined by slits cast by a fan.

Where are they, the old negatives, glass plate and film, she unearthed toward the end? Here, found, ones she scratched, poured salt and sugar on, superimposed with parsley, kernels of corn. As if returning to faces she'd known when she was young, she could begin again.

An illusion, she understood, being a Surrealist. Still, she was comforted by her *curiosités*. A plaster virgin. Suitcase labeled Passenger Markovitch. A scrap of paper stained brown on which she'd written Blood of Picasso. And another piece penciled in blue: Dora, Dora, Dora, Dora, Dora still visible under the dust.

Basilisk

from The Ashmole Bestiary, *1511*

A serpent with cinder wings, a bird's head
and burnt orange body,
the basilisk in *The Ashmole Bestiary*
could vanquish antagonists with a glance.

When we turned sixty, friends and I
celebrated our birthdays in the Caribbean.
Every morning we were roused, I swear, by a basilisk—
this creature was more than a rooster.

He'd been put there, we were sure, to enrage us.
His battle cry started at 5 a.m.,
after which he'd strut up to our glass door
at breakfast and peck furiously to get our attention.

As a basilisk, he could have scorched us
with his glinty eyes, and worse.
Legend is he could reduce onlookers to ashes—
a state we already imagined at our age—

but, defying expectation, we lived
to see in the basilisk what we had become.
How at last we were unafraid
to look anything in the face.

On a Few Lines by Rilke

You come and go. The doors swing closed
ever more gently, almost without a shudder.

Today when you walked with help
from your wheelchair to the bench
I was sitting on, I remembered the first
time you pulled yourself up
and walked to me without falling.

Did it seem a billion years
in the dark when you fell
so far down it may as well have been
the wavy depths where life began?

Another billion before you surfaced.
Opened one blurry eye.

No longer threatened or threatening,
of all who move
through Mercy's quiet rooms
you are the quietest.

Loci

A method that can be used to locate the dead,
    and was, famously, by Simonides,
who named those buried in the ruins

    of a great hall after its roof collapsed
in Thessaly. One nobleman at the end
    of the table, another next—

the poet remembered
    where each sat at the banquet
and, so, led families to their lost.

    His memory palace in ruins
since a fall, I help my son
    read the walls

that surround the booth
    where we've ordered a meal—
barely legible *notae* on knotty pine:

    who loved whom over and over,
palimpsests that obscure
    the whens and ends

until a single year, for him,
    comes into focus,
and they return—*locis et imaginibus.*

    It was upstairs, he says.
And, together, we begin an excavation
    that takes us to a classroom

with a chalkboard, books, friends,
    and the one, he adds, who taught him.
Her name? Her name? It's forgotten

along with years of unhappiness,
accidents, arrests, the illness,
        an acid, that etched his mind.

It was nice in that room, he says.
        It was nice, we say together.
And for the life of us

        in Carbondale, Illinois'
Leaning Tower of Pizza
        we can't remember anything else.

A Flight of Stairs

I can't see where the stairs lead
in a photo I've found
taken of me as a young woman.

Outside, I'm leaning against a railing,
halfway down. A colorless day.
About to rain.

I hardly seem myself in those flared jeans
and secondhand jacket,
long hair down my back.

Beyond this frame:
the men I'll marry.
The children I will bear, unseen.

I'm still counting
those worn, stone steps
rising and falling.

Atlantic grey,
they could be waves
breaking to begin again.

Notes

The book's epigraph by Rainer Maria Rilke is from Anita Barrows' and Joanna Macy's translation of poem I,6 in Rilke's *Book of Hours* (published by Penguin's Riverhead Books, 2005). Also from that book are the epigraph in "On a Few Lines By Rilke" and its final two lines, which are slightly modified (I,45).

The epigraph for "Ménerbes" is from a translation of René Char's "The Library Is On Fire" by Mary Ann Caws (*The Brooklyn Rail*, December 14, 2007).

E. Allison Peers' translation of *Interior Castle* by St. Teresa of Avila (Dover edition) was an important source for "The Seven Chambers of Teresa of Avila's *Interior Castle.*"

For information essential in my writing of poems on Dora Maar, I am grateful to the following authors and their books: *Picasso: Life With Dora Maar* by Anne Baldassari (Flammarion, 2006); *Dora Maar, With and Without Picasso* by Mary Ann Caws (Thames and Hudson, 2000); and *Dora Maar: Prisonnière du regard* by Alicia Dujovne Ortiz (Grasset and Fasquelle, 2003).

In writing "Maria Sibylla Merian's Metamorphoses," I am indebted to Kim Todd for her biography: *Chrysalis: Maria Sibylla Merian and the Secrets of Metamorphosis* (Harcourt, 2007). An extraordinary woman, Merian (1647-1717), an artist and naturalist, was the author of a number of books, including *The Caterpillar's Wondrous Metamorphosis* (1679) and *Metamorphosis of the Insects of Surinam* (1705). The later book includes her drawings of South American insects unknown to European naturalists in her time. She undertook groundbreaking fieldwork in entomology and, using her skills as an artist, painted watercolors that beautifully documented caterpillars in their habitats and their development into butterflies and moths.

Acknowledgments

Grateful acknowledgment is made to the editors of the journals in which these poems first appeared, some times in different versions: *Beloit Poetry Journal, Cincinnati Review, Delaware Poetry Review, Image, New Ohio Review, Poetry Review* (UK), *Shenandoah,* and *The Journal.*

I am deeply thankful for a fellowship to the Dora Maar House in Ménerbes, France, funded by the Brown Foundation. I am also grateful to Southern Illinois University Edwardsville, which provided me with grants that gave me time to write.

The support of dear friends who are writers, especially Jennifer Atkinson, Stacey Lynn Brown, John Burnside, Howard Levy, Cleopatra Mathis, Eric Pankey, and Jane Wayne, was vital to me in the writing of this book. My greatest debt is to my first reader and husband, George Soule.

About the Author

Allison Funk is the author of four previous books of poems, including, most recently, *The Tumbling Box*. The recipient of a fellowship from the National Endowment for the Arts, the Samuel French Morse Poetry Prize, and the Society of Midland Authors Poetry Prize, she is a Distinguished Professor of English at Southern Illinois University Edwardsville.

Photograph of the author by
Salvatore Cincotta. Used by permission.

Free Verse Editions

Edited by Jon Thompson

13 ways of happily by Emily Carr
Between the Twilight and the Sky by Jennie Neighbors
Blood Orbits by Ger Killeen
The Bodies by Chris Sindt
The Book of Isaac by Aidan Semmens
Canticle of the Night Path by Jennifer Atkinson
Child in the Road by Cindy Savett
Condominium of the Flesh by Valerio Magrelli, translated by Clarissa
    Botsford
Contrapuntal by Christopher Kondrich
Country Album by James Capozzi
The Curiosities by Brittany Perham
Current by Lisa Fishman
Dismantling the Angel by Eric Pankey
Divination Machine by F. Daniel Rzicznek
Erros by Morgan Lucas Schuldt
The Forever Notes by Ethel Rackin
The Flying House by Dawn-Michelle Baude
Instances: Selected Poems by Jeongrye Choi, translated by Brenda
    Hillman, Wayne de Fremery, & Jeongrye Choi
The Magnetic Brackets by Jesús Losada, translated by Michael Smith
    & Luis Ingelmo
A Map of Faring by Peter Riley
No Shape Bends the River So Long by Monica Berlin & Beth Marzoni
Pilgrimly by Siobhan Scarry
Physis by Nicolas Pesque, translated by Cole Swensen
Poems from above the Hill & Selected Work by Ashur Etwebi, translated
    by Brenda Hillman & Diallah Haidar
The Prison Poems by Miguel Hernández, translated by Michael Smith
Puppet Wardrobe by Daniel Tiffany
Quarry by Carolyn Guinzio
remanence by Boyer Rickel
Signs Following by Ger Killeen
Split the Crow by Sarah Sousa
Summoned by Guillevic, translated by Monique Chefdor
Sunshine Wound by L. S. Klatt

66

These Beautiful Limits by Thomas Lisk

An Unchanging Blue: Selected Poems 1962–1975 by Rolf Dieter
Brinkmann, translated by Mark Terrill

Under the Quick by Molly Bendall

Verge by Morgan Lucas Schuldt

The Wash by Adam Clay

We'll See by George Godeau, translated by Kathleen McGookey

What Stillness Illuminated by Yermiyahu Ahron Taub

Winter Journey [Viaggio d'inverno] by Attilio Bertolucci, translated by
Nicholas Benson

Wonder Rooms by Allison Funk

CPSIA information can be obtained at www.ICGtesting.com
Printed in the USA
LVOW11s1516160116

470928LV00002B/42/P